The Big Picture Bible Verses

The Big Picture

BIBLE VERSES

Tracing the Storyline of the Bible

David R. Helm

CROSSWAY

WHEATON, ILLINOIS

The Big Picture Bible Verses:
Tracing the Storyline of the Bible

Copyright © 2014 by Holy Trinity Church

Published by Crossway
          1300 Crescent Street
          Wheaton, Illinois 60187

Cover illustration: Gail Schoonmaker

First printing 2014

Printed in the United States of America

Scripture quotations are from the ESV® Bible (*The Holy Bible, English Standard Version®*), copyright © 2001 by Crossway. 2011 Text Edition. Used by permission. All rights reserved.

Trade paperback ISBN: 978-1-4335-4221-3
ePub ISBN: 978-1-4335-4224-4
PDF ISBN: 978-1-4335-4222-0
Mobipocket ISBN: 978-1-4335-4223-7

Library of Congress Cataloging-in-Publication Data
Helm, David R., 1961–
   The big picture bible verses: tracing the storyline of the bible / David Helm.
     pages cm
   ISBN 978-1-4335-4221-3 (pbk.)
   1. Bible—Commentaries—Miscellanea. 2. Catechetics.
3. Christian education of children. 4. Christian education—Home training. I. Title.
BS491.3.H45   2014
268—dc23   2014006267

Crossway is a publishing ministry of Good News Publishers.

VP		24	23	22	21	20	19	18	17	16	15	14
15	14	13	12	11	10	9	8	7	6	5	4	3	2	1

Contents

A Note for Families

Everyone loves stories, and the Bible is a book of stories. However, what many of us miss is that the Bible tells us one story—the story of the activity of God in human history. This catechism is written to help children and adults grow in their understanding and love of the big picture of the Bible.

Part 1

God Creates His Kingdom

Question 1

Q. **Who created the heavens and the earth?**

A. In the beginning, God created the heavens and the earth. (Genesis 1:1)

Question 2

Q. **Who created people?**

A. God created man in his own image, in the image of God he created him; male and female he created them. (Genesis 1:27)

Question 3

Q. **Was God pleased with everything he had made?**

A. God saw everything that he had made, and behold, it was very good. (Genesis 1:31)

Question 4

Q. What command did God give his people to obey?

A. [From] the tree of the knowledge of good and evil you shall not eat, for in the day that you eat of it you shall surely die. (Genesis 2:17)

Question 5

Q. Did God's people obey God's word?

A. [Eve] took of its fruit and ate, and she also gave some to her husband who was with her, and he ate. (Genesis 3:6)

Question 6

Q. How did God judge the Serpent?

A. I will put enmity between you and the woman, and between your offspring and her offspring; he shall bruise your head, and you shall bruise his heel. (Genesis 3:15)

Question 7

Q. How did the Lord God judge his people?

A. The LORD God sent [them] out from the garden of Eden. (Genesis 3:23)

Question 8

Q. What did God see on the earth?

A. God saw the earth, and behold, it was corrupt, for all flesh had corrupted their way on the earth. (Genesis 6:12)

Question 9

Q. How did God promise to judge everything on the earth?

A. I will bring a flood of waters upon the earth to destroy all flesh. (Genesis 6:17)

Part 2

God Begins His Promise

Question 10

Q. How did the Lord begin his promise to rescue all peoples on earth?

A. The LORD said to Abra[ham], "Go . . . to the land that I will show you. And I will make of you a great nation, and I will bless you . . . and in you all the families of the earth shall be blessed." (Genesis 12:1–3)

Question 11

Q. How did Abraham respond to the Lord's word?

A. [Abraham] believed the LORD, and he counted it to him as righteousness. (Genesis 15:6)

Question 12

Q. **What name did God give to Abraham's family?**

A. God said . . . , "Israel shall be your name." (Genesis 35:10)

Question 13

Q. **What happened to Israel in Egypt?**

A. [The Egyptians] set taskmasters over them. . . . But the more they were oppressed, the more they multiplied. (Exodus 1:11–12)

Question 14

Q. **What sign did God use to rescue Israel?**

A. The blood shall be a sign for you. . . . And when I see the blood, I will pass over you. (Exodus 12:13)

Question 15

Q. **What commands did God give Israel to obey?**

A. You shall have no other gods before me. . . . You shall not make for yourself a carved image. . . . You shall not take the name of the LORD your God in vain. . . . Remember the Sabbath day, to keep it holy. . . . Honor your father and your mother. . . . You shall not murder. You shall not commit adultery. You shall not steal. You shall not bear false witness against your neighbor. You shall not covet. . . . (Exodus 20:3–17)

Question 16

Q. What kind of life did God call Israel to live?

A. You shall be holy to me, for I the LORD am holy and have separated you from the peoples, that you should be mine. (Leviticus 20:26)

Question 17

Q. Did Israel promise to obey the Lord their God as King?

A. Speak to us all that the LORD our God will [say], and we will hear and do it. (Deuteronomy 5:27)

Question 18

Q. Did the Lord keep his promises to Israel?

A. Not one word of all the good promises that the LORD had made to the house of Israel had failed; all came to pass. (Joshua 21:45)

Part 3

God Continues His Promise

Question 19

Q. Did Israel keep their promises to God?

A. The LORD said . . . , "They have rejected me
from being king over them." (1 Samuel 8:7)

Question 20

Q. How was God's rule over Israel restored?

A. They anointed David king over Israel.
(2 Samuel 5:3)

Question 21

**Q. Did God say his promise was fulfilled
when David became king?**

A. I will raise up your offspring after you
. . . and I will establish his kingdom.
(2 Samuel 7:12)

Question 22

Q. Did Solomon say God's promise was fulfilled when the temple was built?

A. The highest heaven cannot contain you; how much less this house that I have built! (1 Kings 8:27)

Question 23

Q. How did the nations respond to God's promise?

A. The kings of the earth set themselves, and the rulers take counsel together, against the LORD and against his Anointed. (Psalm 2:2)

Question 24

Q. What did God say about Israel's response to his promise?

A. Children have I reared and brought up, but they have rebelled against me. (Isaiah 1:2)

Question 25

Q. How did the Lord God judge his people this time?

A. Therefore my people [will] go into exile. (Isaiah 5:13)

Question 26

Q. Did God promise to rescue his people from exile?

A. I will bring you back to the place from which I sent you into exile. (Jeremiah 29:14)

Question 27

Q. How will God make it possible for his people to follow him as King?

A. I will give you a new heart, and a new spirit I will put within you. (Ezekiel 36:26)

Part 4

Jesus Fulfills
God's Promise

Question 28

Q. How did the angel introduce Jesus as
   God's promised King?

A. I bring you good news of a great joy that
   will be for all the people. For unto you is
   born this day in the city of David a Savior,
   who is Christ the Lord. (Luke 2:10–11)

Question 29

Q. How did John the Baptist introduce
   Jesus?

A. Behold, the Lamb of God, who takes away
   the sin of the world! (John 1:29)

Question 30

Q. What did Jesus say would prove he was God's promised King?

A. Destroy this temple, and in three days I will raise it up. (John 2:19)

Question 31

Q. What must one do to see God's kingdom?

A. Unless one is born again he cannot see the kingdom of God. (John 3:3)

Question 32

Q. How is one born again into God's kingdom?

A. Jesus said . . . , "I am the resurrection and the life. Whoever believes in me, though he die, yet shall he live." (John 11:25)

Question 33

Q. Who is the only way to God?

A. Jesus said . . . , "I am the way, and the truth, and the life. No one comes to the Father except through me." (John 14:6)

Question 34

Q. How was the way to God opened by Jesus?

A. They crucified him. (John 19:18)

Question 35

Q. Did Jesus say God's promise was fulfilled when he was crucified?

A. [Jesus] said, "It is finished." (John 19:30)

Question 36

Q. How did Thomas respond to Jesus after the resurrection?

A. Thomas answered him, "My Lord and my God!" (John 20:28)

Part 5

God Completes
His Promise

Question 37

Q. How did Jesus say word of his victory
would spread?

A. You will receive power when the Holy
Spirit has come upon you, and you will be
my witnesses in Jerusalem and in all Judea
and Samaria, and to the end of the earth.
(Acts 1:8)

Question 38

Q. What message did Peter spread?

A. [Jesus] is the one appointed by God to be
judge of the living and the dead. To him all
the prophets bear witness that everyone
who believes in him receives forgiveness
of sins through his name. (Acts 10:42–43)

Question 39

Q. **What message did Paul spread?**

A. [Jesus] was delivered up for our trespasses and raised for our justification. (Romans 4:25)

Question 40

Q. **How do we obey God's word?**

A. For by grace you have been saved through faith. And this is not your own doing; it is the gift of God, not a result of works, so that no one may boast. (Ephesians 2:8–9)

Question 41

Q. **What kind of life is God calling us to live?**

A. God has not called us for impurity, but in holiness. (1 Thessalonians 4:7)

Question 42

Q. **How do we know if we are in Christ?**

A. We have come to share in Christ, if indeed we hold our original confidence firm to the end. (Hebrews 3:14)

Question 43

Q. What promise will complete the rescue of God's people?

A. We are waiting for new heavens and a new earth in which righteousness dwells. (2 Peter 3:13)

Question 44

Q. Who receives the glory for completing God's promise?

A. To the only God, our Savior, through Jesus Christ our Lord, be glory, majesty, dominion, and authority, before all time and now and forever. Amen. (Jude 25)

Question 45

Q. What will Jesus say when God's promise is complete?

A. Behold, the dwelling place of God is with man. He will dwell with them, and they will be his people, and God himself will be with them as their God. (Revelation 21:3)

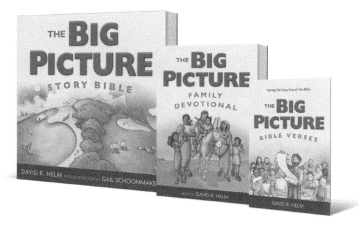

THE BIG PICTURE

STORY BIBLE SERIES

Explore God's Word together as a family with *The Big Picture
Story Bible* and see the big picture of God's love for you unfold
from Genesis to Revelation. Teach your kids to apply God's Word
with *The Big Picture Family Devotional* and help them memorize
key Scripture passages with *The Big Picture Bible Verses.*

Download a free audio recording of The Big Picture Story Bible, *read by the author, at* BigPictureStoryBible.com

crossway.org